Introduction

The Islamic Revolutionary Guard Corps (IRGC), an Iranian military organization, threatens the United States' national interests, energy security, and stability in the Middle East. The Islamic Republic of Iran maintains two separate ground forces, the IRGC (*Sepah-e Pasdaran*) and the regular army (*Artesh*). The *Sepah-e Pasdaran* operates parallel to the *Artesh*, performs domestic security operations, and conducts special operations beyond the Iranian borders. These special operations threaten the stability of Lebanon, Israel, Iraq, Saudi Arabia, and Bahrain because the IRGC sponsors insurgent groups such as Hezbollah, Jaysh al-Mahdi, and Hamas. Additionally, the IRGC controls Iran's nuclear weapons program, which endangers both regional order and US national interests because the international community, including the United States, depends on crude oil from this region for energy security. The IRGC, an organization that perceives the United States as the most significant threat to the Iranian regime, also has the ability to interfere with international shipping operations within the Strait of Hormuz. The Islamic Revolutionary Guard Corps threatens the United States' national interests and stability in and beyond the Middle East because the IRGC controls Iran's nuclear program and sponsors terrorism. This paper analyzes the threat the IRGC's nuclear weapon program and the IRGC's sponsorship of militant Islamic groups pose to the international community and assesses possible US government responses, including multilateral sanctions, regional alliances, covert action, and military action.

Origins

After the Islamic Revolution in 1979, Ayatollah Ruhollah Khomeini established the IRGC and revised the Iranian constitution in accord with his political philosophy.[1] He advocated the *velayat-e faqih*, the doctrinal basis for an Islamic theocratic government. Khomeini

developed his political philosophy based upon his interpretation of Islam and his political

experiences.[2] He concluded that the clergy should establish an Iranian theocracy because the

clergy had superior knowledge of the laws of God; thus, he claimed that the regime of

Mohammed Reza Pahlavi, the Iranian Shah between 1941 and 1979, was abhorrent to Islam.[3]

Khomeini, the clergy, and numerous political organizations overthrew the Shah's regime in

1979.[4] Khomeini created the IRGC before he accepted a formal office in the Iranian

government. He selected members of the *Fadayan-e Islam*, Islamic extremists, and the

Mojahedin-e Khalgh, Islamic Marxists, to protect his ideology and agenda. Many of these

individuals were members of Iran's lower middle class. Some of these militants had conducted

urban guerrilla operations against the Shah's military for many years.[5]

After the Islamic Revolution, Khomeini assumed the role of the Supreme Leader of Iran

and the IRGC became the protectors of a totalitarian Islamic regime. Khomeini became Iran's

absolute religious and political leader. Since he did not trust the *Artesh* to protect his regime and

ideology, the IRGC secured the establishment of the Islamic Republic during a period of post-

revolutionary uncertainty.[6] Once Khomeini secured his position as the Supreme Leader of Iran,

he revised the Iranian constitution to include the roles and responsibilities of the IRGC. Former

members of "underground extremist Islamic and revolutionary leftist organizations" protected

his regime against domestic threats, such as ethnic separatists and social Marxists.[7]

Development

The IRGC developed a military structure during the Iran-Iraq War of 1980-1988. During

the war, the Revolutionary Guard conducted military operations, functioned as a paramilitary force that operated parallel to the conventional armed forces, and maintained domestic security.[8] In September 1980, Saddam Hussein attacked Iran to contain Khomeini's revolution and seize control of the Shatt al-Arab waterway, a region that had strategic importance for Iraq's economy. The waterway connects the confluence of the Tigris and Euphrates rivers to the Persian Gulf.[9] Iraq's seizure of the Shatt al-Arab region would have provided unrestricted access from Basra, the primary Iraqi commercial port, to the Persian Gulf.[10]

Saddam Hussein's invasion allowed the Iranian religious leadership and the IRGC to gain a solid grip on power because the Iranians scrapped reform and dissent in the name of national unity.[11] The Iranian leadership used nationalism as an efficient rallying cry for the war. Khomeini, the IRGC, and their supporters displayed their objectives as a rightful Islamic fight against Iraq's secular regime.[12] The IRGC developed sufficient unity, cohesiveness, and a conventional order of battle that included separate air, ground, and naval services. [13] The IRGC trained and led the *Sepah-e Basij*, the militia forces, to prosecute the war with Iraq.[14] During military operations, the IRGC frequently sacrificed tactical efficiency in exchange for preserving its role as the zealous guardian of the Islamic Revolution. This zealous attitude resulted in the unnecessary sacrifice of thousands of Basij while conducting human wave attacks against Iraqi defensive positions. In the name of religion, the IRGC and the Basij conducted numerous assaults against Iraqi defensive positions that achieved minimal tactical or strategic effects for Iranian military operations.[15] During and after the war, the IRGC protected the principles of Khomeini's government, maintained public order at demonstrations, dislodged other guerrilla factions, suppressed uprisings, provided internal security, gathered human intelligence, and provided military support to prosecute the war with Iraq. Once the war ended, the IRGC solidified its grip on military, political, and economic power. [16]

Structure and Capabilities

The IRGC has a complex structure that addresses both external and internal threats.[17] The IRGC has an estimated force of 125,000 men of which 100,000 of these men are within the IRGC ground force.[18] The other members of the IRGC serve in the naval branch, air branch, and the Qods Force.[19] The ground forces consist of twelve to fifteen divisions deployed in eleven security regions in Iran.[20] There are also separate infantry, armor, and artillery units.[21] Most IRGC divisions have conventional formations such as brigades, battalions, and companies; however, these units are significantly smaller than comparable formations in the US Army. For example, each IRGC division has approximately 4,000 personnel (equivalent to the size of a US Army infantry brigade).[22] Since the IRGC has overall responsibility for protecting the Islamic Revolution, the IRGC has headquarters for the ground forces in all Iranian provinces and urban centers.[23]

In early 1983, the IRGC established specialized air and naval elements.[24] The IRGC Air Force (IRGCAF) provides lift capability for the IRGC's rapid reaction units and provides close air support to IRGC units. The IRGCAF has ten SU-25 Frogfoot attack aircraft and maintains an additional number of fixed wing aircraft such as the Brazilian EMB-312 Tucanos and the Swiss PC-7 for close air support.[25] The IRGC operates a sizeable rotary-wing force consisting of Mi-171 Hip helicopters. The Revolutionary Guard also operates several IL-76 and AN-74T-200 aircraft for troop and equipment transport. The IRGCAF also controls several Iranian built Ababil and Mohajer unmanned aerial vehicles for reconnaissance support.[26] Since Iran does not receive maintenance support from the original manufacturers of its weapon systems, Iran experiences problems maintaining an aging fleet of military aircraft.[27] Iran could resist an US military invasion by depending upon an integrated air defense network and strategic depth to protect air assets.[28]

The surface-to-surface (SSM) missile assets within the IRGCAF are a threat to US forces within the region because the IRGCAF operates Iran's Shahab-3 intermediate-range ballistic missile units.[29] The Shahab-3 units have the ability to attack targets at a range of 1,300 kilometers allowing them to reach targets in Turkey, Saudi Arabia, Iraq, Jordan, and Israel. The IRGCAF received these long range missile capabilities from the North Korea government. There is a strong relationship between the IRGC and the North Korean government that includes the transfer of missile technology.[30] The North Koreans supplied the IRGC with Scud missiles and the Shahab-3 is an Iranian version of the North Korean Nodong missile.[31] During 2006, the North Koreans supplied the IRGC with a missile, the Musudan, which has a range of 1,562 miles.[32] The IRGC operates Iran's SSM missiles and provides the military leadership for all weapons of mass destruction.[33]

The IRGC navy poses a threat to naval forces within the Strait of Hormuz because the IRGC navy has 40 Boghammer fast attack boats and 10 Hudong patrol boats equipped with Saccade anti-ship missiles.[34] The IRGC navy also operates a few submarines and several other small patrol vessels.[35] The IRGC navy has many bases in the Gulf, many near key shipping channels, and some near the Strait of Hormuz.[36] Their preferred tactic is small boat swarm attacks within the Strait of Hormuz, when an enemy ship is at its most vulnerable position.[37] The IRGC also controls Iran's coastal defense forces, including naval guns and an HV-3 Seersucker land-based anti-ship missile unit deployed along the Persian Gulf.[38] The IRGC could mount a significant attack on any island or offshore facility in the Persian Gulf.[39] Additionally, the IRGC could conduct maritime operations in the Strait of Homuz that could threaten the economies of the international community. These maritime operations could disrupt the flow of twenty to thirty percent of the world's oil exports (17 million barrels a day) through the Strait of Hormuz.[40]

The IRGC maintains a unit called the Qods (Jerusalem) Force that conducts terrorists operations, unconventional warfare, and foreign intelligence operations. Several members of the Qods Force serve as unconventional warfare operators and advisors for Islamic insurgents; however, the current force strength for the Qods force is unavailable.[41] The Qods Force is divided regionally into directorates for North America, Europe, North Africa, Iraq, Lebanon, Israel, Palestine, Jordan, Afghanistan, Pakistan, India, Turkey, and the republics of the former Soviet Union.[42] Members of the Qods Force also serve in unofficial positions in Iranian embassies and Iranian businesses.[43] The Qods Force is the primary vehicle for Iran's lethal activities in Iraq because the Qods Force provides weapons, training, funding, and guidance to selected Islamic militants. The Qods Force also provides improvised explosives devices (IED) with explosively formed projectiles (EFP) to Hezbollah and Jaysh al-Mahdi.[44] These weapons pose a significant threat for coalition forces.

Political and Economic Influence

The IRGC seeks to influence and shape Iranian policy in the Middle East. The members of the IRGC are committed to Khomeini's *velayat-e faqih*, articulate their values in a religious context, and protect a small group of elite clerics. The Iranian regime administers the Revolutionary Guard through a structure that is parallel to the *Artesh*. The IRGC commander, Major General Mohammad Ali Ja'fari, reports directly to Ayatollah Ali Hoseyni Khamene'i, the current Supreme Leader of Iran.[45] The IRGC has a strong commitment to its Islamic ideology and serves as the enforcer of Khamene'i policies; however, Iran's clerical elites base their right to rule on Khomeini's ideology, which does not represent the Shi'i mainstream. [46] For example, most Shi'i grand ayatollahs do not accept or support the political philosophy, *velayat-e faqih*; however, the Iranian regime discourages religious dissent or organized opposition groups in politics.[47] The complex nature of Iranian politics and the decentralized method of power sharing allow IRGC commanders to act autonomously. The Iranian regime supports the tactical decisions of the IRGC commanders and will not reverse the actions of the IRGC commanders.[48] For example, these units have full authority to suppress antigovernment sentiment, detain political activists, and suppress protest.[49] Since IRGC units act independently against internal and external enemies, these commanders understand that they have the authority to operate independently of the government in particular situations.[50]

The IRGC has obtained and maintained significant political, military, economic, and religious influence. Since 2004, many former members of the IRGC gained positions within the legislative branch, numerous city councils, and town councils.[51] A group associated with the IRGC also controls the major state-sponsored media.[52] Even Mahmoud Ahmadinejad, the current president of the Islamic Republic of Iran, was a member of the IRGC. In the early 1980s, Ahmadinejad worked in the IRGC's Internal Security Department and conducted covert operations in Kirkuk, Iraq during the Iran-Iraq War. He also served as a senior commander within the elite Qods Force of the IRGC and has provided a significant amount of funding to the IRGC nuclear weapon program.[53] The IRGC uses the nuclear confrontation with the West to influence the Iranian government and maintain political power.[54] The IRGC will soon "dominate political, economic, and cultural life while preserving the regime from domestic threats."[55]

The IRGC has also established itself as an economic force in the country. It controls a vast array of military industries such as the Ammunition and Metallurgy Industries Group, the

Karaj Nuclear Research Center, the Parchin Chemical Industries, and the Ya Mahdi Industries Group. The IRGC has developed several contracting organizations to operate Iran's covert trading networks and to purchase military parts.[56] These economic ventures have helped establish the IRGC's independence while financing security programs. The members of the IRGC maintain economic investments, protect national interests, have high-profile political roles, and define Iran's security interests.[57] Since 1997, Khamene'i has supported the IRGC's growing influence on foreign policy, strategic thinking, and the economy.[58] For example, the IRGC has developed its own military-diplomatic relationships with North Korea, Syria, and China. This level of influence provides the IRGC with the first choice among certain arms purchases, including missiles, fast patrol boats, and submarines.[59]

Nuclear Weapons Program

The IRGC's pursuit of nuclear technology and uranium enrichment capabilities pose a serious challenge to security within a volatile region.[60] General Ja'fari, the commander of the IRGC, is responsible for the nuclear weapon program and will soon have access to highly enriched uranium for nuclear missiles.[61] The IRGC believes nuclear weapons will increase Iran's global influence and reduce Western intervention in the Middle East; therefore, a nuclear weapon would provide the Iranians with significant leverage to influence the nations within the region.[62] Nuclear weapon technology would be dangerous in the hands of a religiously zealous and extremist group such as the IRGC. Since Iran's development of missile and nuclear technology continues, the IRGC will eventually have the ability to equip their missile units with nuclear warheads. If this happens, the IRGCAF will have the ability to target US military forces and assets within the Middle East. There are a few worst case scenarios for this situation, such as an IRGC nuclear strike against Israel or an Israeli nuclear strike against Iran. Additionally, a fanatic IRGC commander or scientist could transfer nuclear material to terrorist organizations or Islamic militants. Islamic militants' access to nuclear material for a "dirty bomb" or nuclear weapon threatens the United States vital interests.

Iran's quest for nuclear weapons presents a security challenge within the Middle East. Iran has invested heavily in nuclear industries during the last 20 years; however, many nuclear facilities within Iran are still incomplete. The Iranians have sought outside help for uranium enrichment facilities, which will provide Iran's self-sufficiency to acquire a nuclear weapon within the next decade.[63] A successful nuclear weapons program in Iran could undermine the Nuclear Non-Proliferation Treaty (NPT) and trigger nuclear weapon production in Saudi Arabia, Egypt, and Turkey.[64] These countries have the capital and capability to acquire or build their own nuclear weapons. Several countries feel threatened by Iran's nuclear weapon program and President Ahmadinejad's recent statements. Ahmadinejad has threatened to destroy Israel with nuclear weapons in public statements, though he lacks constitutional authority to establish the foreign policy or select military targets for the Iranian regime.[65] The US government has the comfort of ignoring these threats; however, the Israeli government cannot assume that Ahmadinejad has made these statements in jest because a nuclear armed IRGC would become a threat to Israel's existence.[66] Since the Iranian regime's policies regarding nuclear weapons are a primary source of political and military tension within the region, Iran's effort to enrich uranium and produce nuclear weapons threatens its amiable existence in the international community.

Support to Insurgents and Militants

The IRGC's sponsorship of insurgent and terrorist groups within the Middle East is a threat to the United States, Lebanon, Israel, and Iraq. Khomeini's objective to export the revolution to other countries, utilizing Islamic ideology, has affected long-term stability in the Middle East.[67] Vice President Joseph Biden stated "Iran's perceived expansionism, including its support for Hezbollah and Hamas, has sparked deep fears, not merely in Israel, but across the Arab world."[68] The IRGC's export of the revolution includes overt military or political support of Islamic revolutionaries, violent activities directed against the United States, and covert action against conservative Arab governments and regime opponents.[69] The IRGC has been the "most active sponsor of international terrorism" and the export of Khomeini's Islamic Revolution.[70] For example, the IRGC provides material and technical support to Islamic militants such as Lebanese Hezbollah, Jaysh al-Mahdi, and Hamas.[71] During the last decade, Iran has become the leading financial supporter for Hamas and Hezbollah.[72] Additionally, Iran has been able to maintain a high degree of regional credibility as a nation "willing to stand up to Israel" because insurgent groups provide Iran with a tool to maintain influence in the Middle East.[73]

There is no evidence that Hamas, Jaysh al-Mahdi, or the Lebanese Hezbollah receives direct orders from Iran. These organizations are self-centered and internally managed groups; however, Iran's material, logistical, and technical support grants Iran a significant amount of influence.[74] For instance, the IRGC still runs terrorist training camps in Lebanon for Hamas and Hezbollah.[75] General Ali Reza Tamzar, the commander for the IRGC unit in Lebanon's Beka'a Valley, conducted and financed training for short-range Fajr-5 missiles and the SA-7 antiaircraft rockets. The IRGC training which also included underwater suicide operations cost the Iranian government $50 million annually.[76]

The IRGC is an autonomous organization that could cause significant harm within the Middle East. The Guard has frequently undertaken actions that clearly conflicted with the policy goals of several of its civilian superiors during the Iran-Iraq War and operations in Lebanon.[77]

The IRGC has dedicated logistical support and military training to Shi'i opposition groups in Iraq, Bahrain, Kuwait, and Saudi Arabia.[78] The ethnic, religious, political, and economic challenges in these areas could "ignite a physical conflict."[79] Tension between Iran and Saudi Arabia are growing because Iran and Saudi Arabia are on opposite sides of a growing Sunni-Shi'i rift that extends from Lebanon through Iraq to the Gulf States and South Asia.[80] The Iranians have played a traditional leadership role in this region; thus, the IRGC will continue to seek instability within the Middle East to increase the dominance of Iranian influence while reducing US government influence. Current actions by the Iranian regime and the IRGC could result in future conflicts in Lebanon, Israel, Iran, Iraq, Saudi Arabia, Bahrain and Afghanistan.

Lebanese Hezbollah (Party of God)

The IRGC's support to Hezbollah is a threat to stability in Israel and Lebanon because Iran has effectively employed Lebanese Hezbollah during past conflicts with Israel. Iran created and supported the Lebanese Hezbollah throughout the 1980s.[81] In response to the Israeli invasion of Lebanon in 1982, Iran sent an IRCG contingent to Lebanon to direct guerilla operations, support Hezbollah, and create a second Shi'ite theocratic in Lebanon. For example, the IRGC's logistic base in Lebanon in 1988 could support 4,000 Hezbollah militia fighters.[82] The most ideologically radical IRGC leaders have generally led and manned the IRGC's Lebanon contingent.[83] There is an unclear chain of command between the IRGC's Lebanon contingent and the Iranian regime. This uncertainty has led to "substantial disagreements between the IRGC commanders and the leadership in Tehran" over the methods and tactics of the IRGC in Lebanon.[84]

Hezbollah's ability to combine an organized political movement with decentralized armed cells is a threat to stability in Lebanon and Israel. Since Hezbollah has accomplished its "main goal of ousting Israel from southern Lebanon," some members of Hezbollah want the organization to transition from a guerrilla organization into a purely political organization. However, several militants within Hezbollah refuse to coexist with Israel, reject any compromises with the Israeli government, and intend to continue the conflict with the Israeli government.[85] Hassan Nasrallah, the leader of Hezbollah, viewed the departure of Israeli forces from the Gaza strip as a victory for the Palestinian resistance and a validation for Hezbollah's position on the Israeli-Palestinian issue.[86] During 2006, the war between Israel and Hezbollah lasted thirty days. Since Nasrallah rejects blame for the July 2006 war, he claims the Israeli government used the capture of the Israeli soldiers on July 12, 2006 as a pretext to launch its failed campaign of annihilation.[87] Despite Nasrallah's claim of a Hezbollah victory, Israeli military operations in southern Lebanon during 2006 significantly reduced Hezbollah's capability to conduct rocket attacks against Israel and influenced Hezbollah's future militant activity.

The Qods Force provides direct support to a militant organization that frequently employs terrorist tactics such as hostage taking, rocket attacks against civilians, and suicide attacks against civilians. The IRGC will continue to support Hezbollah because it is a strategic asset in critical negotiations to gain concessions from the international community. For example, members of the Reagan administration secretly sold weapons to Iran during the Iran-Iraq War in return for Iran's help in releasing Hezbollah-held hostages in Lebanon.[88] On numerous occasions, the IRGC supplied Hezbollah with multiple ranged rockets to support Hezbollah's 15 year military campaign against Israeli forces in Lebanon and northern Israel.[89]

Hezbollah's ability to employ suicide terrorist tactics is a threat to security in Lebanon and Israel. During the 1980s, Hezbollah pioneered the concept of Muslim suicide bombing.[90] Hezbollah was involved in the suicide bombings of the US Embassy, the US Marine barracks, and the US Embassy annex in Beirut during the 1980s. Under IRGC guidance and direction, Hezbollah attacked these targets.[91] These suicide attacks claimed the lives of 241 American citizens.[92] In 1992, Hezbollah and possibly members of the IRGC conducted terrorist attacks against the Israeli embassy and the Argentine-Jewish Mutual Association in Buenos Aires, Argentina resulting in 86 dead. After the attack, the Argentinean law enforcement agencies arrested 20 members of Hezbollah.[93] About 150 members of the Qods Force remain in Lebanon to coordinate Iran's aid to Hezbollah; the Iranians gave Hezbollah about $100 million per year between 1996 and 2001.[94]

Muqtada Sadr's Jaysh al-Mahdi

The IRGC's support to Muqtada Sadr, a radical Shi'i cleric and Iraqi nationalist, is a threat to stability in Iraq. Muqtada al-Sadr, the surviving son of the revered Ayatollah Mohammed Sadeq al-Sadr and "the voice of the Shi'i resistance," sought support from the Qods Force to support his resistance movement.[95] After the invasion of coalition forces, Iranian leadership recognized an unprecedented opportunity to extend their influence in Iraq. Iran supported Muqtada Sadr because Iranian hardliners feared that a stable democratic Iraq would present an alternative model of government that could undermine their own authority.[96] In addition, Iranian hardliners supported Muqtada al-Sadr's militia, Jaysh al-Mahdi, because the Iranians believed that successful attacks against American forces weakened the will of the Americans to support an invasion of Iran.[97] Detained members of Jaysh al-Mahdi indicated that the Qods Force had supported numerous attacks against coalition and Iraqi forces. The Qods

Force provided small arms, rockets, mortars, and explosives to Jaysh al-Mahdi. [98] After al-Qaeda militants destroyed a Shi'i shrine in Samarra, Iraq; Jaysh al-Mahdi's engagement in sectarian violence posed the greatest threat to long-term stability in Iraq during 2006-2007. [99]

Jaysh al-Mahdi is one of several beneficiaries of IRGC's support within Iraq. The Iranian government supported several political parties within Iraq such as the Supreme Islamic Iraqi Council (SIIC), the al-Dawa party, and the Sadrist Movement. [100] Since Iraq is the only Shi'i-ruled Arab state and Shi'i political domination in Iraq extends Iranian influence in the Middle East, it is in the best interest of the IRGC and the Iranian government to support the Shi'i power brokers in Iraq. The IRGC will use the Jaysh al-Mahdi to attack its perceived threats, the Americans, because successful attacks against coalition forces in Iraq delay any future American plans to invade Iran. [101] Jaysh al-Mahdi was responsible for bombings, extortion, sectarian murders, kidnappings, and other attacks. [102] In August 2008, coalition military operations in southern Iraq disrupted Qods Force and Jaysh al-Mahdi operations. Since the Government of Iraq's objective is to minimize Muqtada al-Sadr's influence in Iraq, several Qods Force operatives and members of Jaysh al-Mahdi fled to Iran to avoid detention. [103]

Hamas

Since Hamas' founding in 1987, the IRGC's support to Hamas has been a threat to Israel. Hamas consists of an extremist militant element and a social services element. [104] During 2006, the Palestinians democratically elected Hamas to govern the Gaza Strip in Israel. After a long history of terrorist attacks, Hamas has achieved some of its political objectives. [105] In contrast to the Iranian regime and Hezbollah, the leaders of Hamas are not religious authorities. [106] Despite sectarian and political differences, the Iranian government is Hamas' most important and explicit state sponsor.[107] During the last conflict between Hamas and Israel from December 27, 2008 to January 20, 2009, the IRGC supplied several long range 122mm rockets to support Hamas' attacks against Israel.[108] Hamas remains an obstacle to the successful resolution of the Israeli-Palestinian peace process because of Hamas' frequent attacks against Israel and Fatah, Hamas's political rival. [109] The conflict between Hamas and Israel has resulted in the deaths of several Palestinians and Israelis.

US Government Responses

The US government's approach to the Iranian threat will require the application of all the instruments of national power, since direct talks with Iranian leadership comes with difficulties and risks.[110] The Iranian leaders are not irrational; however, US government policies and communications must be clear and precise to overcome differences based upon historic suspicion and political stakes.[111] It is also imperative that the international community views Iran's nuclear program as the world's problem. The United Nations Security Council agrees that Iran has sought to deceive the international community about its nuclear intentions; therefore, the international community has condemned the Iranian leadership's decision to move ahead with uranium enrichment. The Iranians have conducted several last minute negotiations to delay nuclear site inspections and split the international community; however, the international community should view Iran's nuclear threats to Israel as an international problem.[112]

Multilateral sanctions are an option to limit Iran's production of nuclear weapons and support to terrorist organizations. Some American politicians have advocated punitive and unilateral sanctions focused on international companies doing business in Iran.[113] However, the US government's reliance on unilateral sanctions has not succeeded.[114] Therefore, the United

States and its allies at the United Nations are seeking multilateral, diplomatic, and economic sanctions.[115] Multilateral economic sanctions have had an impact on the Iranian people and business community; thus, the sanctions must continue to isolate Iran.[116] Additionally, economic and diplomatic failures have diminished President Ahmadinejad's influence.[117] Since Iran needs the support of the international community to deliver oil to the international market and support domestic economic programs, Khamene'i and Ahmadinejad should not let the production of nuclear weapons outweigh the potential profits for economic development.[118] Multilateral economic sanctions will continue to diminish Ahmadinejad and the IRGC's political credibility.

The United States should maintain agreements with allies within the Middle East, develop additional bilateral security agreements with other countries in this region, and provide air defense assets to allies within the region to weaken Iran's influence. American policy in the near term is to build a broad multilateral and international coalition against Iran's nuclear ambitions.[119] It is in the national interest of the United States to provide a mix of air, land, and sea-based theater missile defense systems to US allies within the region to intercept the IRGC's ballistic missiles.[120] The IRGC's Shahab-3 missiles have the capability to fly either low-level or high-altitude trajectories. Since such trajectories are difficult for Patriot air defense assets to intercept, the United States will have to provide defense assets that overcome the limitations of the Patriot air defense system.[121] Alliances and the theater missile defense systems should deter Iranian use of nuclear weapons, if sanctions fail to deter the Iranians.

US military action in Iran is another option to suppress Iran's support of terrorism and prevent Iran from gaining a nuclear weapon capability. In contrast to overt military action, it would be better to influence the Iranian regime with economic sanctions, non-kinetic measures, and covert action because overt military action against Iran will ignite the destructive side of the

Iranian leadership and the nationalistic spirit of the Iranian people. Covert action against nuclear facilities and the Qods Force units entails the least risk of political complications or a harsh Iranian response. The United States should use covert action to disrupt, defeat, or neutralize IRGC units that threaten American allies in the Middle East. Covert operations will require a robust special operations force that includes intelligence assets that support the targeting of nuclear facilities. The human intelligence personnel that support these missions must understand the Iranian culture and nuclear weapon production. Intelligence personnel and covert operatives could sabotage nuclear facilities at dispersed and deeply buried sites such as Iran's enrichment facilities in Natanz and the heavy water plants in Arak.[122] Effective covert action would reduce the risk of Iranian retaliation against the United States because Iranian authorities would not be able to determine whether damage to a nuclear facility was the result of sabotage or an industrial accident.[123] Covert action that limited civilian casualties would also avoid igniting the will of the Iranian people.

US military or Israeli preemptive air strikes would alleviate the requirement to deploy a large military force to topple the regime, destroy the Iranian military, secure the nuclear sites, control Iran's population, restore essential services, and conduct stability operations; however, air strikes may not achieve the necessary objectives. The objectives should be the complete destruction of Iran's nuclear weapons program and a change to Khamene'i stance on nuclear weapons. While the goal of these air strikes would be a drastic change to Khamene'i policy without causing the Iranian citizens to rally to support the Iranian regime and a nationalist cause directed against the United States, it would be very difficult for the US military to conduct a preemptive strike without incurring a large number of civilian deaths. Since several nuclear sites are near civilian population centers, the amount of civilian casualties could be very high.[124]

Additionally, Iran's nuclear facilities are widely dispersed and deeply buried.[125] Attacks against these sites will require long duration bombing, several sorties, and the possible use of nuclear weapons. The US military would have to consider the effects of radiological fallout from these sites and the proximity of these sites to large Iranian cities. Since the effects could be devastating to the Iranian society and economic development, the population could rally to a nationalist cause and this effect would be a significant threat to the US interests within the region.[126] In retaliation, the IRGC could influence its network of militants to attack US interests and military facilities in Iraq, Bahrain, Kuwait, or Qatar.[127] The results of ineffective air strikes could also lead to a major United States-Iran-Israel conflict.

A ground invasion would have several consequences. After two major campaigns in Iraq and Afghanistan, a US military ground invasion as a preemptive measure would have limited support from the American citizens. However, American popular support would be necessary for protracted military operations within Iran. The IRGC would provide an extensive defensive capability in the event of an invasion of Iran.[128] The IRGC gives the Iranian regime a significant asymmetric advantage within the mountainous and urban terrain of Iran.[129] During an invasion of Iran, US military forces would face a professional paramilitary force, the IRGC, which has had 30 years to develop tactics and doctrine for unconventional warfare in mountainous and urban areas. The IRGC can employ small units in mountains terrain, urban regions, and remote areas to counter our advantages in intelligence collection capabilities; therefore, the US military must master irregular warfare in mountainous and urban terrain to defeat the IRGC. The US military's mastery of conventional and irregular warfare would reduce the Revolutionary Guards capabilities; however, a US ground invasion would lead to a protracted conflict in Iran and Iraq. During a ground invasion, the Iranian leadership could encourage the Jasysh al-Mahdi and the

Badr Brigade to attack US forces in retaliation for a ground invasion.[130] The Badr Brigade has long standing ties with the IRGC. Many Badr members have become integrated into the Iraqi security forces, while other members of the Badr Brigade hold government positions in southern Iraq.[131] Muqtada al-Sadr could turn Iraq into a "hell" for the Iraqi citizens and a threat to its neighbors.[132] Iran could also stop oil exports entirely and shut down all oil-tanker traffic within the Persian Gulf, which would cut between twenty-five and thirty-three percent of the world's oil supply.[133]

Conclusion

The Islamic Revolutionary Guard Corps' sponsorship of terrorism, control of Iran's nuclear program, and execution of Iran's national strategy threatens stability within the Middle East. During the last 30 years, the IRGC has emerged as an entity that has limited government oversight, prevailed over other centers of power in Iran, acted as one of the most independent groups in Iran, and exported the Shi'i variety of revolutionary Islam to other countries. The IRGC has opposed US policies in the Middle East since its founding in 1979. During the Iran-Iraq War, the IRGC concurrently fought a war, enforced religious doctrine, and maintained political stability. The IRGC has successfully protected the Iranian regime against external and domestic threats by conducting decentralized operations to achieve the Iranian regime's national strategy. This military organization's goal to spread the Shi'i Islamic revolution within the Middle East has threatened stability within Iraq, Lebanon, and Israel. The United States needs a stable Middle East to maintain international energy requirements. Additionally, stable conditions in this region support the United States' energy security requirements. A nuclear weapon equipped IRGC is a significant risk to the United States and Israel's vital interests. The transfer of nuclear material from a fanatical member of the IRGC to militants such as Hezbollah,

Jaysh al-Mahdi, Hamas, or al-Qaeda would threaten the vital interests and survival of the United States and Israel.

The United States must address the impacts of Iran's nuclear weapons program, Iran's missile arsenal, the concern for Israel's safety, the integrity of Gulf shipping lanes within the Strait of Hormuz, and the possibility of Iranian mobilization of terrorist attacks around the globe. Iranian policies in Iraq, Lebanon, and Israel pose significant challenges to the United States' interests in the region. The geopolitical dynamics, intercontinental ballistic missiles, and the emergence of globalization play a primary role in the understanding of America's security concerns. These issues have changed the United States' perception of what constitutes an immediate threat. Possible US government responses include multilateral sanctions, regional alliances, covert military action, and overt military action.

The IRGC's autonomy, revolutionary rhetoric, and political agenda would be dangerous within a nuclear armed Iran. Currently, the IRGC controls the Iranian nuclear weapon program and their quest for nuclear weapons is a long-term challenge for the United States government. Iran's pursuit of nuclear technology and enrichment capabilities also poses a serious challenge to the United States' strategic partners, Israel and Saudi Arabia. Since the Middle East remains crucial to American security concerns, the US government must consider the IRGC as an immediate threat. The United States government must respond to the IRGC's sponsorship of terrorism and control of the Iranian nuclear program to reduce Iranian aggression, control nuclear weapons proliferation, contain totalitarian Islamism, influence the IRGC, and reduce terrorism.

Appendix A: Khomeini, the Shah, and the Iranian Revolution

Khomeini developed his political philosophy based upon his interpretation of Islam and his political experiences.[134] Khomeini adopted several religious and political principles from Ahmad Naraghi, an Iranian mullah who developed the philosophy in the eighteen century.[135] Khomeini further claimed that the regime of Mohammed Reza Pahlavi, the Iranian Shah between 1941 and 1979, was abhorrent to Islam.[136] Khomeini's *velayat-e faqih* philosophy called for an Islamic government to replace the Iranian monarchy. Khomeini claimed that he was the most knowledgeable and most just among the *mujtahids*; therefore, he claimed to possess the religious and political authority to represent the Twelfth Imam, Mohammad al-Mahdi. This authority would provide his right to serve as the Supreme Ruler of Iran; however, his claim to authority broke one of the Shi'i sect's core tenets, all government in absence of Mohammad al-Mahdi is profane.[137] A major factor in Khomeini's revolutionary politicization of Shi'ism and the success of the Islamic Revolution was his charismatic leadership. Khomeini combined millenarianism, *velayat-e faqih*, and his charisma to convince the Iranian that the Shah's polices were a significant threat to Islam and Iranian traditions.[138] Khomeini supported a revolution that overthrew the Shah in 1979.

The government of Iran was a constitutional monarchy with a parliamentary system, a Shah as the head of state, and a prime minster as the head of government between 1907 and 1953. In March 1951, the Shah accepted Mohammad Mossadeq as the Prime Minister.[139] In 1951, Prime Minster Mohammad Mossadeq, an advocate for democracy in the Iranian parliament, nationalized the British-owned Anglo-Iranian Oil Company, which controlled all of Iran's petroleum resources.[140] In 1952, Mossadeq dissolved the Iranian parliament and the Shah abandoned Iran for self-exile in Europe.[141] The British convinced President Dwight

Eisenhower's administration that Mosaddeq's actions indicated Iran's intent to join the Soviet

Bloc. In accord with the policy of containment, the Eisenhower administration supported an

Iranian military coup during 1953 that reinstated the Shah to the throne after his exile in

Europe.[142]

Once the Shah returned to Iran, he relentlessly strengthened his power to prevent a

repetition of the events of 1953. He limited the freedom of political expression and increased the

capabilities of his internal security organization, the National Intelligence and Security

Organization, to suppress political opposition and dissident activities because the dissident

intelligentsia staged several riots and protests during the 1960s and 1970s.[143] The Shah concerns

were legitimate. For example, the National Intelligence and Security Organization discovered a

Soviet spy ring in "the Iranian army composed of six hundred officers of whom sixty" held ranks

of lieutenant-colonel or higher.[144] The Shah believed that the opposition groups "acted as a

deterrent to Iran's progress."[145] Despite these political challenges, the Shah expanded industry,

widened access to employment, increased the availability of education, and improved economic

opportunities.[146] The Shah modernized Iran's infrastructure and military while developing

strong relationships with Western powers. Khomeini considered the Western powers as a threat

to Islam and Iran. He believed the Western powers would exploit Iran's resources, dilute Islam,

"destroy the reputation of Islamic leaders", and conquer all Islamic countries.[147] Khomeini and

the discontented population viewed the Shah as a puppet of the United States and the Western

powers.[148] The Shah arrested Khomeini on June 4, 1963 for his revolutionary rhetoric and

support to dissident groups. The Shah released Khomeini during the spring of 1964 to quell

violent protests and demonstrations. That same year the Shah sent Khomeini into exile for his opposition of the "White Revolution". Khomeini spent his exile in Iraq, Turkey, and France.[149] By 1967, the Shah survived the Mossadeq era, two assassination attempts, and Ayatollah Khomeini's first challenge to the Shah's regime.[150] The Shah's disregard for domestic issues and concerns eventually resulted in a revolution in 1979. After the Islamic Revolution and upon his return to Iran, Khomeini assumed the role of the Supreme Leader of Iran and the IRGC became the protectors of a totalitarian Islamic regime. The IRGC's primary mission is to control dissent and protect the *vali-ye faqih*.

Appendix B: US Government Sanctions Against Iran

Current sanctions include restrictions and prohibition on aid, non-emergency agricultural aid, economic transactions, loans from United States financial institutions, and support from the international banks system.[151] Economic deprivation forced upon the people of a nation has changed the behavior of nations in the past. Economic sanctions are a "coercive measure to bring about a change in behavior or policies."[152] The utility of sanctions is to pressure Iran to negotiate along the United States' terms. The United States should not "lift or ease sanctions until Iranian policy concerning nuclear weapons and terrorism changes."[153] Multilateral sanctions are necessary for this strategy of economic warfare. Scientific studies conclude United States unilateral economic sanctions are ineffective; while, multilateral sanctions are frequently effective.[154] International organizations, such as the United Nations, are the most effective for economic sanctions because a global organization can isolate the economy of a nation. Other organizations that have the capability to isolate Iran are the World Trade Organization, the World Bank, and the International Monetary Fund.[155]

Unilateral sanctions have been the "mainstay of the United States' strategies" for Iran.[156] The following laws include sanctions against Iran: International Emergency Economic Powers Act, Iran-Libya Sanctions Act of 1996, and Trade Sanctions Reform Act of 2000.[157] Thus far, Iran has not paid a significant price for its violations of its commitments under the Nuclear Non-Proliferation Treaty (NPT) and failure to fully cooperate with the International Atomic Energy Agency (IAEA).[158] US sanctions include restrictions on commercial cooperation, non-emergency agricultural aid, trade, and loans from US financial institutions.[159] Based on Dr. Patrick Clawson's testimony before the US Senate, current sanctions do not include exports of crude oil or imports of gasoline because such sanctions would also affect the price of gasoline and oil within the United States.[160] Sanctions that included the exports of oil would have a significant impact on the world economy. The utility of sanctions is to pressure Iran to agree along United States' terms of negotiation. The United States should not "lift or ease sanctions until Iran's policies concerning terrorism and nuclear weapons changes.[161]

The US government should impose sanctions on Iranian oil exports and gasoline imports prior to the commitment of the US military to air strikes or a unilateral ground invasion. Europe, Russia, and China may not agree to sanctions without the United States conducting direct negotiations with the Iranian regime.[162] Multilateral oil sanction against Iranian would be detrimental to Japan and China. Japan is Iran's largest customer, followed closely by China. Iran trades about thirty three percent of its oil exports with Japan and China; however, the United States does not purchase Iranian oil.[163] Based on China and Japan's dependence on Iranian oil, the US government's partners and allies may block any measures that include sanctions against Iranian oil exports.

Photo Removed Due to Copyright Restrictions

Source:
Adapted from Wilfried Buchta, *Who Rules Iran?* (Washington: The Washington Institute for Near East Policy and the Konrad Adenauer Stiftung, 2000).

Photo Removed Due to Copyright Restrictions

Source:
Adapted from Wilfried Buchta, *Who Rules Iran?* (Washington: The Washington Institute for Near East Policy and the Konrad Adenauer Stiftung, 2000).

Photo Removed Due to Copyright Restrictions

Sources:
Wilfried Buchta, *Who Rules Iran?* (Washington: The Washington Institute for Near East Policy and the Konrad Adenauer Stiftung, 2000).

Said Arjomand, *The Turban for the Crown: The Islamic Revolution in Iran.* (New York: Oxford University Press, 1988).

Appendix F: Ranges for Iranian Missiles

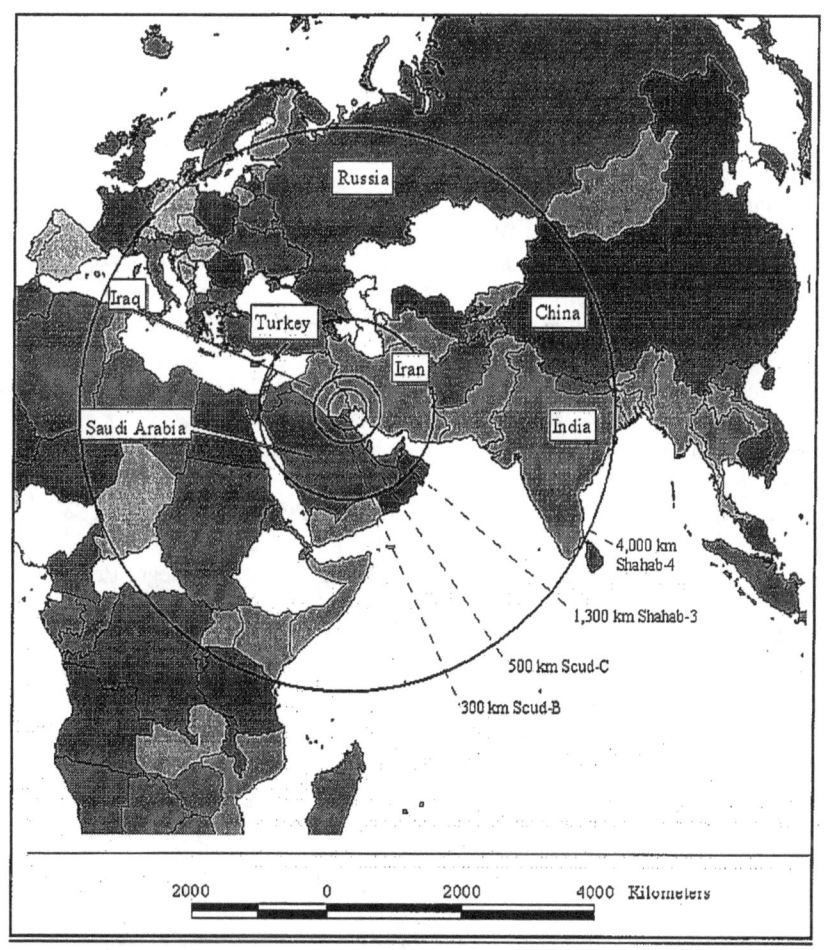

System	Range
Shahab-1 (Scud-B)	300 km
Shahab-2 (Scud-C)	500 km
Shahab-3	1,300 km
Shahab-4	4,000 km

Source:

House Committee on Intelligence, *Recognizing Iran as a Strategic Threat: An Intelligence Challenge for the United States,* 109th Cong., 2nd sess., August 23, 2006, URL: http://intelligence.house.gov/Media/PDFS/IranReport082206v2.pdf.

Notes

[1] U.S. Federal Research Division Library of Congress, *Iran: A Country Study* (Washington, DC: Federal Research Division, 2008), 54-55.

[2] U.S. Federal Research Division Library of Congress, *Iran: A Country Study* (Washington, DC: Federal Research Division, 2008), 45-46.

[3] Ruhollah Khomeini, *Islam and Revolution*, trans. Hamid Algar (Berkely, CA: Mizan Press, 1981), 57-62.

[4] Thomas R. Mattair, *Global Security Watch: Iran* (Westport, CT: Praeger Security International, 2008), 26-28.

[5] Kenneth Katzman, *The Warriors of Islam: Iran's Revolutionary Guard* (Boulder, CO: Westview Press, 1993), 30-31.

[6] Nikola B. Schahgaldian and Gina Barkhordarian, *The Iranian Military Under the Islamic Republic* (Santa Monica, CA: RAND Corporation, 1987), 18-19.

[7] Nikola B. Schahgaldian and Gina Barkhordarian, *The Iranian Military Under the Islamic Republic* (Santa Monica, CA: RAND Corporation, 1987), 65.

[8] Nikola B. Schahgaldian and Gina Barkhordarian, *The Iranian Military Under the Islamic Republic* (Santa Monica, CA: RAND Corporation, 1987), 73.

[9] Ronald F. Rokosz, "Clausewitz and the Iraq-Iran War" (individual study project, U.S. Army War College, Carlisle Barracks, 1989), 3.

[10] Stephen R. Grummon, *The Iran-Iraq War: Islam Embattled* (Washington, DC: Praeger Publishers, 1982), 3.

[11] Nathan Gonzales, *Engaging Iran: The Rise of a Middle East Powerhouse and America's Strategic Choice* (Westport, CT: Praeger Security International, 2007), 97-98.

[12] Nathan Gonzales, *Engaging Iran: The Rise of a Middle East Powerhouse and America's Strategic Choice* (Westport, CT: Praeger Security International, 2007), 62.

[13] Kenneth Katzman, *The Warriors of Islam: Iran's Revolutionary Guard* (Boulder, CO: Westview Press, 1993), 86.

[14] Ali Alfoneh, "The Revolutionary Guards' Role in Iranian Politics," *Middle East Quarterly* (Fall 2008), http://www.meforum.org/article/1979 (accessed October 23, 2008).

[15] Stephen C. Pelletiere and Douglas V. Johnson, *Lessons Learned: The Iran-Iraq War* (Carlisle Barracks, PA: Strategic Studies Institute, U.S. Army War College, 1991), 14.

[16] Ali Alfoneh, "The Revolutionary Guards' Role in Iranian Politics," *Middle East Quarterly* (Fall 2008), http://www.meforum.org/article/1979 (accessed October 23, 2008).

[17] Anthony Cordesman, *Iran's Developing Military Capabilities* (Washington, DC: Center for Strategic and International Studies Press, 2005), 45.

[18] International Institute for Strategic Studies, *The Military Balance: 2008* (London, UK: Europa Publications, 2008), 243.

[19] Anthony Cordesman, *Iran's Developing Military Capabilities* (Washington, DC: Center for Strategic and International Studies Press, 2005), 45.

[20] Wilfred Buchta, *Who Rules Iran? The Structure of Power in the Islamic Republic* (Washington, DC: The Washington Institute for Near East Policy, 2000), 68.

[21] Anthony Cordesman, *Iran's Revolutionary Guards, the Al Quds Force, and Other Intelligence and Paramilitary Forces* (Washington, DC: Center for Strategic and International Studies Press, 2007), 4-6, http://www.csis.org/media/csis /pubs/070816_cordesman_report.pdf (accessed November 1, 2008).

[22] Jane's Information Group, "Iran: Army," *Jane's Sentinel Security Assessment – The Gulf States* (January, 2009), http://www4.janes.com (Accessed February 17, 2009).

[23] Nikola B. Schahgaldian and Gina Barkhordarian, *The Iranian Military Under the Islamic Republic* (Santa Monica, CA: RAND Corporation, 1987), 64.

[24] Nikola B. Schahgaldian and Gina Barkhordarian, *The Iranian Military Under the Islamic Republic* (Santa Monica, CA: RAND Corporation, 1987), 73.

[25] Fariborz Haghshenass, "Iran's Air Forces: Struggling to Maintain Readiness," *Policy Watch* 1066 (December 22, 2005). http://www.washingtoninstitute.org/templateC05.php?CID=2422 (Accessed February 18, 2009).

[26] Fariborz Haghshenass, "Iran's Air Forces: Struggling to Maintain Readiness," *Policy Watch* 1066 (December 22, 2005). http://www.washingtoninstitute.org/templateC05.php?CID=2422 (Accessed February 18, 2009).

[27] Fariborz Haghshenass, "Iran's Air Forces: Struggling to Maintain Readiness," *Policy Watch* 1066 (December 22, 2005). http://www.washingtoninstitute.org/templateC05.php?CID=2422 (Accessed February 18, 2009).

[28] Fariborz Haghshenass, "Iran's Air Forces: Struggling to Maintain Readiness," *Policy Watch* 1066 (December 22, 2005). http://www.washingtoninstitute.org/templateC05.php?CID=2422 (Accessed February 18, 2009).

[29] Anthony Cordesman, *Iran's Developing Military Capabilities* (Washington, DC: Center for Strategic and International Studies Press, 2005), 46.

[30] Bruce Bechtol, *Red Rogue: The Persistent Challenge of North Korea* (Washington, DC: Potomac Books Incorporated, 2007) 47-48.

[31] Alireza Jafarzadeeh, *The Iran Threat: President Ahmadinejad and the Coming Nuclear Crisis* (New York, NY: Palgrave MacMillan, 2007), 178-179.

[32] Larry Niksch, *North Korea: Terrorism List Removal?*, CRS Report for Congress RL30613 (Washington, DC: Congressional Research Service, July 10, 2008), 29.

[33] Anthony Cordesman, *Iran's Developing Military Capabilities* (Washington, DC: Center for Strategic and International Studies Press, 2005), 47.

[34] Matthew M. Frick, "Iran's Islamic Revolutionary Guard Corps: An Open Source Analysis." *Joint Forces Quarterly* 49 (2nd Quarter 2008): 122.

[35] International Institute for Strategic Studies, *The Military Balance: 2008* (London, UK: Europa Publications, 2008), 243.

[36] Anthony Cordesman, *Iran's Developing Military Capabilities* (Washington, DC: Center for Strategic and International Studies Press, 2005), 45.

[37] Matthew M. Frick, "Iran's Islamic Revolutionary Guard Corps: An Open Source Analysis." *Joint Forces Quarterly* 49 (2nd Quarter 2008): 122.

[38] Anthony Cordesman, *Iran's Developing Military Capabilities* (Washington, DC: Center for Strategic and International Studies Press, 2005), 45.

[39] Anthony Cordesman, *Iran's Developing Military Capabilities* (Washington, DC: Center for Strategic and International Studies Press, 2005), 48.

[40] Robert S. Strauss Center for International Security and Law, *The Strait of Hormuz: Political-Military Analysis of Threats to Oil Flows* (Austin, TX: Lyndon B. Johnson School of Public Affairs, 2008), 1-3, http://www.robertstrausscenter.org/img/upload/1219257530_PRP%20final.pdf (accessed January 20, 2009).

[41] Anthony Cordesman, *Iran's Revolutionary Guards, the Al Quds Force, and Other Intelligence and Paramilitary Forces* (Washington, DC: Center for Strategic and International Studies Press, 2007), 8, http://www.csis.org/media /csis /pubs/070816_cordesman_report.pdf (accessed November 1, 2008).

[42] Nathan Gonzales, *Engaging Iran: The Rise of a Middle East Powerhouse and America's Strategic Choice* (Westport, CT: Praeger Security International, 2007), 98.

[43] Anthony Cordesman, *Iran's Developing Military Capabilities* (Washington, DC: Center for Strategic and International Studies Press, 2005), 46.

[44] Senate Committee on Foreign Relations, *Iran: An Update: Hearing before the Committee on Foreign Relations*, 110th Cong., 1st sess., March 29, 2007, 40.

[45] Ali Alfoneh, "The Revolutionary Guards' Role in Iranian Politics," *Middle East Quarterly* (Fall 2008), http://www.meforum.org/article/1979 (accessed October 23, 2008).

[46] Kenneth Katzman, *The Warriors of Islam: Iran's Revolutionary Guard* (Boulder, CO: Westview Press, 1993), 139.

[47] Wilfred Buchta, *Who Rules Iran? The Structure of Power in the Islamic Republic* (Washington, DC: The Washington Institute for Near East Policy, 2000), 88-94.

[48] Ali Ansari, *Confronting Iran: The Failure of American Foreign Policy and the Next Great Crisis in the Middle East* (New York: Perseus Books Group, 2006), 220.

[49] Wilfred Buchta, *Who Rules Iran? The Structure of Power in the Islamic Republic* (Washington, DC: The Washington Institute for Near East Policy, 2000), 67.

[50] Ali Ansari, *Confronting Iran: The Failure of American Foreign Policy and the Next Great Crisis in the Middle East* (New York: Perseus Books Group, 2006), 220.

[51] Anoushiravan Ehteshami and Mahjoob Zweiri, *Iran and the Rise of its Neoconservatives: The Politics of Tehran's Silent Revolution* (New York: IB Tauris and Company Limited Company, 2007), 82.

[52] Anthony Cordesman, *Iran's Developing Military Capabilities* (Washington, DC: Center for Strategic and International Studies Press, 2005), 46.

[53] Anoushiravan Ehteshami and Mahjoob Zweiri, *Iran and the Rise of its Neoconservatives: The Politics of Tehran's Silent Revolution* (New York: IB Tauris and Company Limited Company, 2007), 55.

[54] Anoushiravan Ehteshami and Mahjoob Zweiri, *Iran and the Rise of its Neoconservatives: The Politics of Tehran's Silent Revolution* (New York: IB Tauris and Company Limited Company, 2007), 82.

[55] Mehdi Khalaji. "Iran's Revolutionary Guards, Inc," *Policy Watch* 1273, (August 17, 2007) http://www.washingtoninstitute.org/ templateC05.php?CID=2649 (accessed February 18, 2009).

[56] Anthony Cordesman, *Iran's Revolutionary Guards, the Al Quds Force, and Other Intelligence and Paramilitary Forces* (Washington, DC: Center for Strategic and International Studies Press, 2007), 11, http://www.csis.org/media /csis /pubs/070816_cordesman_report.pdf (accessed November 1, 2008).

[57] Anoushiravan Ehteshami and Mahjoob Zweiri, *Iran and the Rise of its Neoconservatives: The Politics of Tehran's Silent Revolution* (New York: IB Tauris and Company Limited Company, 2007), 82.

[58] Anoushiravan Ehteshami and Mahjoob Zweiri, *Iran and the Rise of its Neoconservatives: The Politics of Tehran's Silent Revolution* (New York: IB Tauris and Company Limited Company, 2007), 82.

[59] Shahram Chubin, *Iran's National Security Policy: Capabilities, Intentions, and Impact* (Washington, DC: The Carnegie Endowment for International Peace, 1994), 32.

[60] U.S. Department of Defense, *National Defense Strategy*, Arlington, VA: Department of Defense, 2008, 1-3.

[61] Senate Committee on Foreign Relations, *Iran's Political / Nuclear Ambitions and U.S. Policy Options: Hearings before the Committee on Foreign Relations*, 109th Cong., 2nd sess., May 17, 2006 and May 18, 2006, 18.

[62] Senate Committee on Foreign Relations, *Iran's Political / Nuclear Ambitions and U.S. Policy Options: Hearings before the Committee on Foreign Relations*, 109th Cong., 2nd sess., May 17, 2006 and May 18, 2006, 43.

[63] Thomas R. Mattair, *Global Security Watch: Iran* (Westport, CT: Praeger Security International, 2008), 82.

[64] Senate Committee on Foreign Relations, *Iran's Political / Nuclear Ambitions and U.S. Policy Options: Hearings before the Committee on Foreign Relations*, 109th Cong., 2nd sess., May 17, 2006 and May 18, 2006, 18.

[65] Senate Committee on Foreign Relations, *Iran: An Update: Hearing before the Committee on Foreign Relations*, 110th Cong., 1st sess., March 29, 2007, 1.

[66] U.S. Department of Defense, *National Defense Strategy*, Arlington, VA: Department of Defense, 2008, 9.

[67] Nathan Gonzales, *Engaging Iran: The Rise of a Middle East Powerhouse and America's Strategic Choice* (Westport, CT: Praeger Security International, 2007), 62.

[68] Senate Committee on Foreign Relations, *Iran: An Update: Hearing before the Committee on Foreign Relations*, 110th Cong., 1st sess., March 29, 2007, 1.

[69] Michael Rubin, "Iran's Revolutionary Guards – A Rogue Outfit?" *Middle East Quarterly* (Fall 2008), http://www.meforum.org/article/1990 (accessed October 23, 2008).

[70] Kenneth Katzman, *Terrorism: Near Eastern Groups and State Sponsors, 2002*, CRS Report for Congress RL31119 (Washington, DC: Congressional Research Service, February 13, 2002), 30.

[71] Nathan Gonzales, *Engaging Iran: The Rise of a Middle East Powerhouse and America's Strategic Choice* (Westport, CT: Praeger Security International, 2007), 101.

[72] Senate Committee on Foreign Relations, *Iran: An Update: Hearing before the Committee on Foreign Relations*, 110th Cong., 1st sess., March 29, 2007, 31.

[73] Nathan Gonzales, *Engaging Iran: The Rise of a Middle East Powerhouse and America's Strategic Choice* (Westport, CT: Praeger Security International, 2007), 91.

[74] Nathan Gonzales, *Engaging Iran: The Rise of a Middle East Powerhouse and America's Strategic Choice* (Westport, CT: Praeger Security International, 2007), 101.

[75] Matthew Levitt, *Hamas: Politics, Charity, and Terrorism in the Service of Jihad* (New Haven, CT: Yale University Press, 2006), 177.

[76] Matthew Levitt, *Hamas: Politics, Charity, and Terrorism in the Service of Jihad* (New Haven, CT: Yale University Press, 2006), 177.

[77] Kenneth Katzman, *The Warriors of Islam: Iran's Revolutionary Guard* (Boulder, CO: Westview Press, 1993), 138.

[78] Wilfred Buchta, *Who Rules Iran? The Structure of Power in the Islamic Republic* (Washington, DC: The Washington Institute for Near East Policy, 2000), 70.

[79] Senate Committee on Foreign Relations, *Iran: An Update: Hearing before the Committee on Foreign Relations*, 110th Cong., 1st sess., March 29, 2007, 1-2.

[80] Senate Committee on Foreign Relations, *Iran: An Update: Hearing before the Committee on Foreign Relations*, 110th Cong., 1st sess., March 29, 2007, 1-2.

[81] Nathan Gonzales, *Engaging Iran: The Rise of a Middle East Powerhouse and America's Strategic Choice* (Westport, CT: Praeger Security International, 2007), 64.

[82] John Poole, *Tactics of the Crescent Moon: Militant Muslim Combat Methods* (Emerald Isle, NC: Posterity Press, 2004), 31.

[83] Kenneth Katzman, *The Warriors of Islam: Iran's Revolutionary Guard* (Boulder, CO: Westview Press, 1993), 96.

[84] Kenneth Katzman, *The Warriors of Islam: Iran's Revolutionary Guard* (Boulder, CO: Westview Press, 1993), 96-97.

[85] Kenneth Katzman, *Terrorism: Near Eastern Groups and State Sponsors, 2002*, CRS Report for Congress RL31119 (Washington, DC: Congressional Research Service, February 13, 2002), 5.

[86] Joseph Alagha, *The Shifts in Hizbullah's Ideology: Religious Ideology, Political Ideology, and Political Program* (Leiden, Netherlands: Amsterdam University Press, 2002), 66.

[87] Augustus Norton, *Hezbollah: A Short History* (Princeton, NJ: Princeton University Press, 2007), 154.

[88] Nathan Gonzales, *Engaging Iran: The Rise of a Middle East Powerhouse and America's Strategic Choice* (Westport, CT: Praeger Security International, 2007), 101.

[89] Kenneth Katzman, *Terrorism: Near Eastern Groups and State Sponsors, 2002*, CRS Report for Congress RL31119 (Washington, DC: Congressional Research Service, February 13, 2002), 5.

[90] Jeroen Gunning, *Hamas in Politics: Democracy, Religion, Violence* (New York, NY: Columbia University, 2008), 47.

[91] Augustus Norton, *Hezbollah: A Short History* (Princeton, NJ: Princeton University Press, 2007), 71.

[92] Kenneth Katzman, *Terrorism: Near Eastern Groups and State Sponsors, 2002*, CRS Report for Congress RL31119 (Washington, DC: Congressional Research Service, February 13, 2002), 5.

[93] Kenneth Katzman, *Terrorism: Near Eastern Groups and State Sponsors, 2002*, CRS Report for Congress RL31119 (Washington, DC: Congressional Research Service, February 13, 2002), 6.

[94] Kenneth Katzman, *Terrorism: Near Eastern Groups and State Sponsors, 2002*, CRS Report for Congress RL31119 (Washington, DC: Congressional Research Service, February 13, 2002), 6.

[95] Gwynne Dyer, *After Iraq: Anarchy and Renewal in the Middle East* (New York, NY: Thomas Dunne Books, 2007), 26.

[96] Zbigniew Brzezinski, Robert M. Gates, and Suzanne Maloney, *Iran: Time for a New Approach* (New York: Council on Foreign Relations, 2004), 26.

[97] Senate Committee on Foreign Relations, *Iran: An Update: Hearing before the Committee on Foreign Relations*, 110th Cong., 1st sess., March 29, 2007, 40.

[98] Senate Committee on Foreign Relations, *Iran: An Update: Hearing before the Committee on Foreign Relations*, 110th Cong., 1st sess., March 29, 2007, 40.

[99] James A. Baker and others, *The Iraq Study Group Report* (New York: Vintage Books, 2006), 4.

[100] Gwynne Dyer, *After Iraq: Anarchy and Renewal in the Middle East* (New York, NY: Thomas Dunne Books, 2007), 26.

[101] Senate Committee on Foreign Relations, *Iran: An Update: Hearing before the Committee on Foreign Relations*, 110th Cong., 1st sess., March 29, 2007, 40.

[102] Senate Committee on Foreign Relations, *Iran: An Update: Hearing before the Committee on Foreign Relations*, 110th Cong., 1st sess., March 29, 2007, 40.

[103] Multi-National Forces-Iraq, *Measuring Stability and Security in Iraq: December 2008 Report to Congress* (Baghdad, Iraq: Department of Defense, 2009), 18-19, http://www.defenselink.mil/pubs/pdfs/9010_Report_to_Congress_Dec_08.pdf (accessed January 30, 2009).

[104] Kenneth Katzman, *Terrorism: Near Eastern Groups and State Sponsors, 2002*, CRS Report for Congress RL31119 (Washington, DC: Congressional Research Service, February 13, 2002), 7.

[105] Jeroen Gunning, *Hamas in Politics: Democracy, Religion, Violence* (New York, NY: Columbia University, 2008), 1.

[106] Jeroen Gunning, *Hamas in Politics: Democracy, Religion, Violence* (New York, NY: Columbia University, 2008), 107.

[107] Matthew Levitt, *Hamas: Politics, Charity, and Terrorism in the Service of Jihad* (New Haven, CT: Yale University Press, 2006), 172.

[108] Anthony Cordesman, *The "Gaza War": A Strategic Analysis* (Washington, DC: Center for Strategic and International Studies Press, 2009), 8. http://www.csis.org/media/csis/pubs/090202_gaza_war.pdf (accessed February 10, 2009).

[109] Jeroen Gunning, *Hamas in Politics: Democracy, Religion, Violence* (New York, NY: Columbia University, 2008), 2.
[110] Senate Committee on Foreign Relations, *Iran's Political / Nuclear Ambitions and U.S. Policy Options: Hearings before the Committee on Foreign Relations*, 109th Cong., 2nd sess., May 17, 2006 and May 18, 2006, 1.
[111] Senate Committee on Foreign Relations, *Iran's Political / Nuclear Ambitions and U.S. Policy Options: Hearings before the Committee on Foreign Relations*, 109th Cong., 2nd sess., May 17, 2006 and May 18, 2006, 2.
[112] Senate Committee on Foreign Relations, *Iran: An Update: Hearing before the Committee on Foreign Relations*, 110th Cong., 1st sess., March 29, 2007, 1-2.
[113] Senate Committee on Foreign Relations, *Iran's Political / Nuclear Ambitions and U.S. Policy Options: Hearings before the Committee on Foreign Relations*, 109th Cong., 2nd sess., May 17, 2006 and May 18, 2006, 2.
[114] Zbigniew Brzezinski, Robert M. Gates, and Suzanne Maloney, *Iran: Time for a New Approach* (New York: Council on Foreign Relations, 2004), 3.
[115] Senate Committee on Foreign Relations, *Iran's Political / Nuclear Ambitions and U.S. Policy Options: Hearings before the Committee on Foreign Relations*, 109th Cong., 2nd sess., May 17, 2006 and May 18, 2006, 1.
[116] Senate Committee on Foreign Relations, *Iran: An Update: Hearing before the Committee on Foreign Relations*, 110th Cong., 1st sess., March 29, 2007, 2.
[117] Senate Committee on Foreign Relations, *Iran: An Update: Hearing before the Committee on Foreign Relations*, 110th Cong., 1st sess., March 29, 2007, 2.
[118] Alidad Mafinezam and Aria Mehrabi, *Iran and Its Place Among Nations* (Westport, CT: Praeger Publishers, 2008), 93.
[119] Senate Committee on Foreign Relations, *Iran's Political / Nuclear Ambitions and U.S. Policy Options: Hearings before the Committee on Foreign Relations*, 109th Cong., 2nd sess., May 17, 2006 and May 18, 2006, 1.
[120] Senate Committee on Foreign Relations, *Iran's Political / Nuclear Ambitions and U.S. Policy Options: Hearings before the Committee on Foreign Relations*, 109th Cong., 2nd sess., May 17, 2006 and May 18, 2006, 108.
[121] Patrick Clawson and Michael Eisenstadt, "Opportunities and Challenges for U.S. Policy," In *Iran Under Khatami* (Washington, DC: The Washington Institute for Near East Policy, 1998), 80.
[122] Shahram Chubin, *Iran's Nuclear Ambitions* (Washington, DC: The Carnegie Endowment for International Peace, 2006), 25.
[123] Patrick Clawson and Michael Eisenstadt, *The Last resort: Consequences of Preventive Military Action Against Iran* (Washington, DC: The Washington Institute for Near East Policy, 2008), 14.
[124] Patrick Clawson and Michael Eisenstadt, *The Last resort: Consequences of Preventive Military Action Against Iran* (Washington, DC: The Washington Institute for Near East Policy, 2008), 14-15.
[125] Gwynne Dyer, *After Iraq: Anarchy and Renewal in the Middle East* (New York, NY: Thomas Dunne Books, 2007), 74.
[126] Patrick Clawson and Michael Eisenstadt, *The Last resort: Consequences of Preventive Military Action Against Iran* (Washington, DC: The Washington Institute for Near East Policy, 2008), 8-9.
[127] Patrick Clawson and Michael Eisenstadt, *The Last resort: Consequences of Preventive Military Action Against Iran* (Washington, DC: The Washington Institute for Near East Policy, 2008), 19.
[128] Anthony Cordesman, *Iran's Developing Military Capabilities* (Washington, DC: Center for Strategic and International Studies Press, 2005), 47.
[129] Anthony Cordesman, *Iran's Developing Military Capabilities* (Washington, DC: Center for Strategic and International Studies Press, 2005), 45.
[130] Gwynne Dyer, *After Iraq: Anarchy and Renewal in the Middle East* (New York, NY: Thomas Dunne Books, 2007), 75.
[131] James A. Baker and others, *The Iraq Study Group Report* (New York: Vintage Books, 2006), 5.
[132] Gwynne Dyer, *After Iraq: Anarchy and Renewal in the Middle East* (New York, NY: Thomas Dunne Books, 2007), 105.
[133] Gwynne Dyer, *After Iraq: Anarchy and Renewal in the Middle East* (New York, NY: Thomas Dunne Books, 2007), 75.
[134] U.S. Federal Research Division Library of Congress, *Iran: A Country Study* (Washington, DC: Federal Research Division, 2008), 45-46.
[135] Alireza Jafarzadeeh, *The Iran Threat: President Ahmadinejad and the Coming Nuclear Crisis* (New York, NY: Palgrave MacMillan, 2007), 48.
[136] Ruhollah Khomeini, *Islam and Revolution*, trans. Hamid Algar (Berkely, CA: Mizan Press, 1981), 57-58.

[137] Sandra Mackey, *The Iranians: Persia, Islam and the Soul of a Nation* (New York: Penguin Group, 1996), 233.

[138] Said Arjomand, *The Turban for the Crown: The Islamic Revolution in Iran* (New York: Oxford University Press, 1988), 100.

[139] Thomas R. Mattair, *Global Security Watch: Iran* (Westport, CT: Praeger Security International, 2008), 8-12.

[140] U.S. Federal Research Division Library of Congress, *Iran: A Country Study* (Washington, DC: Federal Research Division, 2008), 32-33.

[141] Thomas R. Mattair, *Global Security Watch: Iran* (Westport, CT: Praeger Security International, 2008), 11-12.

[142] Nathan Gonzales, *Engaging Iran: The Rise of a Middle East Powerhouse and America's Strategic Choice* (Westport, CT: Praeger Security International, 2007), 5.

[143] George Lenczowski, "Political Process and Institutions in Iran: The Second Pahlavi Kingship," *Iran Under the Pahlavis*, ed. George Lenczowski (Stanford, CA: Hoover Institution Press, 1978), 451-459.

[144] George Lenczowski, "Political Process and Institutions in Iran: The Second Pahlavi Kingship," *Iran Under the Pahlavis*, ed. George Lenczowski (Stanford, CA: Hoover Institution Press, 1978), 451.

[145] George Lenczowski, "Political Process and Institutions in Iran: The Second Pahlavi Kingship," *Iran Under the Pahlavis*, ed. George Lenczowski (Stanford, CA: Hoover Institution Press, 1978), 461.

[146] U.S. Federal Research Division Library of Congress, *Iran: A Country Study* (Washington, DC: Federal Research Division, 2008), 32-33.

[147] Ruhollah Khomeini, *Islam and Revolution*, trans. Hamid Algar (Berkely, CA: Mizan Press, 1981), 139-142.

[148] Nathan Gonzales, *Engaging Iran: The Rise of a Middle East Powerhouse and America's Strategic Choice* (Westport, CT: Praeger Security International, 2007), 5.

[149] Sandra Mackey, *The Iranians: Persia, Islam and the Soul of a Nation* (New York: Penguin Group, 1996), 227.

[150] Sandra Mackey, *The Iranians: Persia, Islam and the Soul of a Nation* (New York: Penguin Group, 1996), 230.

[151] Jeremy Sharp, *Lebanon: The Israel-Hamas-Hezbollah Conflict*, CRS Report for Congress RL33566 (Washington, DC: Congressional Research Service, September 15, 2006), 45.

[152] Hossein G. Askari, John Forrer, Hidly Teegen, and Jiawen Yang, *Economic Sanctions: Examining Their Philosophy and Efficacy* (Westport, CT: Praeger Security International, 2003), 14-15.

[153] Patrick Clawson and Michael Eisenstadt, "Opportunities and Challenges for U.S. Policy," In *Iran Under Khatami* (Washington, DC: The Washington Institute for Near East Policy, 1998), 106-108.

[154] Hossein G. Askari, John Forrer, Hidly Teegen, and Jiawen Yang, *Economic Sanctions: Examining Their Philosophy and Efficacy* (Westport, CT: Praeger Security International, 2003), 31.

[155] Hossein G. Askari, John Forrer, Hidly Teegen, and Jiawen Yang, *Economic Sanctions: Examining Their Philosophy and Efficacy* (Westport, CT: Praeger Security International, 2003), 32-33.

[156] Meghan L. O'Sullivan, *Shrewd Sanctions: Statecraft and State Sponsors of Terrorism* (Washington, DC: Brookings Institution Press, 2003), p. 45.

[157] Jeremy Sharp, *Lebanon: The Israel-Hamas-Hezbollah Conflict*, CRS Report for Congress RL33566 (Washington, DC: Congressional Research Service, September 15, 2006), 41-42.

[158] Senate Committee on Foreign Relations, *Iran's Political / Nuclear Ambitions and U.S. Policy Options: Hearings before the Committee on Foreign Relations*, 109th Cong., 2nd sess., May 17, 2006 and May 18, 2006, 102.

[159] Jeremy Sharp, *Lebanon: The Israel-Hamas-Hezbollah Conflict*, CRS Report for Congress RL33566 (Washington, DC: Congressional Research Service, September 15, 2006), 45.

[160] Senate Committee on Foreign Relations, *Iran's Political / Nuclear Ambitions and U.S. Policy Options: Hearings before the Committee on Foreign Relations*, 109th Cong., 2nd sess., May 17, 2006 and May 18, 2006, 58-65.

[161] Patrick Clawson and Michael Eisenstadt, "Opportunities and Challenges for U.S. Policy," In *Iran Under Khatami* (Washington, DC: The Washington Institute for Near East Policy, 1998), 108.

[162] Senate Committee on Foreign Relations, *Iran's Political / Nuclear Ambitions and U.S. Policy Options: Hearings before the Committee on Foreign Relations*, 109th Cong., 2nd sess., May 17, 2006 and May 18, 2006, 4.

[163] Senate Committee on Foreign Relations, *Iran's Political / Nuclear Ambitions and U.S. Policy Options: Hearings before the Committee on Foreign Relations*, 109th Cong., 2nd sess., May 17, 2006 and May 18, 2006, 99.

Bibliography

Alagha, Joseph. *The Shifts in Hizbullah's Ideology: Religious Ideology, Political Ideology, and Political Program*. Leiden, Netherlands: Amsterdam University Press, 2002.

Alfoneh, Ali. "The Revolutionary Guards' Role in Iranian Politics." *Middle East Quarterly* (Fall 2008). http://www.meforum.org/article/1979 (accessed October 23, 2008).

Ansari, Ali. *Confronting Iran: The Failure of American Foreign Policy and the Next Great Crisis in the Middle East*. New York: Perseus Books Group, 2006.

Arjomand, Said. *The Turban for the Crown: The Islamic Revolution in Iran*. New York: Oxford University Press, 1988.

Askari, Hossein G., John Forrer, Hidly Teegen, and Jiawen Yang. *Economic Sanctions: Examining Their Philosophy and Efficacy*. Westport, CT: Praeger Security International, 2003.

Baker, James A., Lee H. Hamilton, Lawrence S. Eagleburger, Vernon E. Jordan, Edwin Meese III, Sandra Day O'Connor, Leon E. Panetta, William J. Perry, Charles S. Robb, and Alan K. Simpson. *The Iraq Study Group Report*. New York: Vintage Books, 2006.

Bechtol, Bruce. *Red Rogue: The Persistent Challenge of North Korea*. Washington, DC: Potomac Books Incorporated, 2007.

Brzezinski, Zbigniew, Robert M. Gates, and Suzanne Maloney. *Iran: Time for a New Approach*. New York: Council on Foreign Relations, 2004.

Buchta, Wilfred. *Who Rules Iran? The Structure of Power in the Islamic Republic*. Washington, DC: The Washington Institute for Near East Policy, 2000.

Caudill, Shannon W. "Hizballah Rising: Iran's Proxy Warriors." *Joint Forces Quarterly* 49 (2nd Quarter 2008): 128-134.

Chubin, Shahram. *Iran's National Security Policy: Capabilities, Intentions, and Impact*. Washington, DC: The Carnegie Endowment for International Peace, 1994.

Chubin, Shahram. *Iran's Nuclear Ambitions*. Washington, DC: The Carnegie Endowment for International Peace, 2006.

Clawson, Patrick and Michael Eisenstadt. "Opportunities and Challenges for U.S. Policy." In *Iran Under Khatami*, 99-114: Washington, DC: The Washington Institute for Near East Policy, 1998.

Clawson, Patrick and Michael Eisenstadt. *The Last Resort: Consequences of Preventive Military Action Against Iran*. Washington, DC: The Washington Institute for Near East Policy, 2008.

Cordesman, Anthony. *Iran's Developing Military Capabilities*. Washington, DC: Center for Strategic and International Studies Press, 2005.

Cordesman, Anthony. *The "Gaza War": A Strategic Analysis*. Washington, DC: Center for Strategic and International Studies Press, 2009. http://www.csis.org/media/csis/pubs/090202_gaza_war.pdf (accessed February 10, 2009).

Cordesman, Anthony. *Iran's Revolutionary Guards, the Al Quds Force, and Other Intelligence and Paramilitary Forces*. Washington, DC: Center for Strategic and International Studies Press, 2007. http://www.csis.org/media/csis/pubs/070816_cordesman_report.pdf (accessed November 1, 2008).

Dyer, Gwynne. *After Iraq: Anarchy and Renewal in the Middle East*. New York, NY: Thomas Dunne Books, 2007.

Ehteshami, Anoushiravan and Mahjoob Zweiri. *Iran and the Rise of its Neoconservatives: The Politics of Tehran's Silent Revolution*. New York: IB Tauris and Company Limited Company, 2007.

Frick, Matthew M. "Iran's Islamic Revolutionary Guard Corps: An Open Source Analysis." *Joint Forces Quarterly* 49 (2nd Quarter 2008): 121-127.

Gonzales, Nathan. *Engaging Iran: The Rise of a Middle East Powerhouse and America's Strategic Choice*. Westport, CT: Praeger Security International, 2007.

Grummon, Stephen R. *The Iran-Iraq War: Islam Embattled*. Washington, DC: Praeger Publishers, 1982.

Gunning, Jeroen. *Hamas in Politics: Democracy, Religion, Violence*. New York, NY: Columbia University, 2008.

Haghshenass, Fariborz. "Iran's Air Forces: Struggling to Maintain Readiness." *Policy Watch* 1066, (December 22, 2005). http://www.washingtoninstitute.org/templateC05.php?CID=2422 (accessed February 18, 2009).

International Institute for Strategic Studies. *The Military Balance: 2008*. London, UK: Europa Publications, 2008.

Jafarzadeeh, Alireza. *The Iran Threat: President Ahmadinejad and the Coming Nuclear Crisis*. New York, NY: Palgrave MacMillan, 2007.

Jane's Information Group. "Iran: Army". *Jane's Sentinel Security Assessment – The Gulf States.* (January, 2009). http://www4.janes.com (accessed February 17, 2009).

Karsh, Efraim. *The Iran-Iraq War 1980-1988.* Oxford: Osprey Publishing, 2002.

Katzman, Kenneth. *Iran's Activities and Influence in Iraq.* CRS Report for Congress RS22323. Washington, DC: Congressional Research Service, April 9, 2008.

Katzman, Kenneth. *Iran: U.S. Concerns and Policy Responses.* CRS Report for Congress RL32048. Washington, DC: Congressional Research Service, October 8, 2008.

Katzman, Kenneth. *Terrorism: Near Eastern Groups and State Sponsors, 2002.* CRS Report for Congress RL31119. Washington, DC: Congressional Research Service, February 13, 2002.

Katzman, Kenneth. *The Warriors of Islam: Iran's Revolutionary Guard.* Boulder, CO: Westview Press, 1993.

Khalaji, Mehdi. "Iran's Revolutionary Guards, Inc." *Policy Watch* 1273, (August 17, 2007). http://www.washingtoninstitute.org/templateC05.php?CID=2649 (accessed February 18, 2009).

Khomeini, Ruhollah. *Islam and Revolution.* Translated by Hamid Algar. Berkely, CA: Mizan Press, 1981.

Lenczowski, George. "Political Process and Institutions in Iran: The Second Pahlavi Kingship." In *Iran Under the Pahlavis,* edited by George Lenczowski, 433-475: Stanford, CA: Hoover Institution Press, 1978.

Levitt, Matthew. *Hamas: Politics, Charity, and Terrorism in the Service of Jihad.* New Haven, CT: Yale University Press, 2006.

Mackey, Sandra. *The Iranians: Persia, Islam and the Soul of a Nation.* New York: Penguin Group, 1996.

Mafinezam, Alidad and Aria Mehrabi. *Iran and Its Place Among Nations.* Westport, CT: Praeger Security International, 2008.

Mattair, Thomas R. *Global Security Watch: Iran.* Westport, CT: Praeger Security International, 2008.

Multi-National Forces-Iraq. *Measuring Stability and Security in Iraq: December 2008 Report to Congress.* Baghdad, Iraq: Department of Defense, 2009. http://www.defenselink.mil /pubs/pdfs/9010_Report_to_Congress_Dec_08.pdf (accessed January 30, 2009).

Niksch, Larry. *North Korea: Terrorism List Removal?* CRS Report for Congress RL30613. Washington, DC: Congressional Research Service, July 10, 2008.

Norton, Augustus. *Hezbollah: A Short History.* Princeton, NJ: Princeton University Press, 2007.

O'Sullivan, Meghan L. *Shrewd Sanctions: Statecraft and State Sponsors of Terrorism.* Washington, DC: Brookings Institution Press, 2003.

Pelletiere, Stephen C., and Douglas V. Johnson. *Lessons Learned: The Iran-Iraq War.* Carlisle Barracks, PA: Strategic Studies Institute, U.S. Army War College, 1991.

Poole, John. *Tactics of the Crescent Moon: Militant Muslim Combat Methods.* Emerald Isle, NC: Posterity Press, 2004.

Potter, Lawrence G., and Gary G. Sick. *Iran, Iraq, and the Legacies of War.* New York: Palgrave MacMillan, 2004.

Rokosz, Ronald F. "Clausewitz and the Iraq-Iran War." Individual Study Project, U.S. Army War College, Carlisle Barracks, 1989.

Robert S. Strauss Center for International Security and Law. *The Strait of Hormuz: Political-Military Analysis of Threats to Oil Flows.* Austin, TX: Lyndon B. Johnson School of Public Affairs, 2008. http://www.robertstrausscenter.org/img/upload/ 1219257530_PRP%20final.pdf (accessed January 20, 2009).

Rubin, Michael. "Iran's Revolutionary Guards – A Rogue Outfit?" *Middle East Quarterly* (Fall 2008). http://www.meforum.org/article/1990 (accessed October 23, 2008).

Schahgaldian, Nikola B., and Gina Barkhordarian. *The Iranian Military Under the Islamic Republic.* Santa Monica, CA: RAND Corporation, 1987.

Sharp, Jeremy. *Lebanon: The Israel-Hamas-Hezbollah Conflict.* CRS Report for Congress RL33566. Washington, DC: Congressional Research Service, September 15, 2006.

Streusand, Douglas. "Managing the Iranian Threat to Iranian Sea Commerce Diplomatically." In *Getting Ready for a Nuclear Ready Iran,* edited by Henry Sokolski and Patrick Clawson, 257-283: Carlisle, PA: Strategic Studies Institute, 2005. http://www. strategicstudiesinstitute.army.mil/pdffiles/PUB629.pdf (accessed January 26, 2009).

U. S. Congress. House. Committee on Intelligence. *Recognizing Iran as a Strategic Threat: An Intelligence Challenge for the United States.* 109th Cong., 2nd sess., August 23, 2006. http://intelligence.house.gov/Media/PDFS/IranReport082206v2.pdf (accessed January 26, 2009).

U. S. Congress. Senate. Committee on Foreign Relations. *Iran: An Update: Hearing before the Committee on Foreign Relations.* 110th Cong., 1st sess., March 29, 2007.

U. S. Congress. Senate. Committee on Foreign Relations. *Iran's Political / Nuclear Ambitions and U.S. Policy Options: Hearings* before *the Committee on Foreign Relations.* 109th Cong., 2nd sess., May 17, 2006 and May 18, 2006.

U.S. Central Intelligence Agency. *The World Factbook.* Washington, DC: Central Intelligence Agency, December 18, 2008. https://www.cia.gov/library/publications/the-world-factbook/geos/ir.html (accessed January 10, 2009).

U.S. Department of Defense. *National Defense Strategy.* Arlington, VA: Department of Defense, 2008.

U.S. Federal Research Division Library of Congress. *Iran: A Country Study.* Washington, DC: Federal Research Division, 2008.

www.ingramcontent.com/pod-product-compliance
Lightning Source LLC
Chambersburg PA
CBHW081539280526
45788CB00010B/3288